THE ADULT LEARNER

In A Nutshell

s e r i e s

THE ADULT LEARNER

Some Things We Know

In A Nutshell

collection

Robin J. Fogarty • Brian M. Pete

CORWIN
A SAGE Company

For information:

Corwin
A SAGE Company
2455 Teller Road
Thousand Oaks,
    California 91320
(800) 233-9936
Fax: (800) 417-2466
www.corwinpress.com

SAGE Ltd.
1 Oliver's Yard
55 City Road
London EC1Y 1SP
United Kingdom

SAGE India Pvt. Ltd.
B 1/I 1 Mohan Cooperative
    Industrial Area
Mathura Road,
    New Delhi 110 044
India

SAGE Asia-Pacific Pte. Ltd.
33 Pekin Street #02-01
Far East Square
Singapore 048763

Printed in the United States of America

A catalog record of this book is available from the Library of Congress.

ISBN: 978-0-9747-4163-5

This book is printed on acid-free paper.

09   10   11   12   13   10 9 8 7 6 5 4 3 2 1

Dedication

To Regina Vickary Haig,
        the quintessential student,
        the ultimate adult learner,
        for whom the joy of learning finally kicked into
        high gear!

■ □ ■ □ ■

Contents

■ □ ■ □ ■

Acknowledgments

For their pioneering work in discovering the adult learner...
    Malcomb Knowles
    Ron Zemke and Susan Zemke
    Judy Erin Krupp

For their insightful writings about change theory...
    Michael Fullan
    Tom Guskey

For their ground-breaking efforts in professional development...
    Susan Loukes-Horsely
    Ann Lieberman
    Mike Schmoker
    Bruce Joyce and Beverly Showers

And, last but not least...

For their dedication and talent in producing this book...
    Dara Lee Howard
    Jon Hensley
    Susana Siew-Demunck
    Elaine and David Brownlow

■ □ ■ □ ■

Preface

When it comes to teaching adults, people often ask, "Is it easier to teach adults or kids?" The answer is always an unequivocal; "Kids are easier! Adults get grumpy." Of course, that statement about being grumpy is said with tongue-in-cheek. But the truth of the matter is, it is harder to teach adults.

When teaching adults, the adrenaline is pumping. You are addressing your peers. It's different! It's challenging! It's high stakes! In fact, there is a myth that holds that public speaking is the greatest fear an adult has. It goes on to say that the second greatest fear is death. Now, whether this is fact or fiction, it hints at the perceived level of risk involved when adults speak to peers. Adults teach adults. And, no matter how experienced one is working with the adult learner, a notable level of anxiety is always there.

We have total respect for the species called the adult learner. It's in this view that this piece explains some of the things we know.

Enjoy,

Robin J. Fogarty and Brian M. Pete

Chicago, 2004

Introduction

The Adult Learner: Some Things We Know addresses the "warrior" who rises to the challenge of teaching the adult learner. The discussion is designed as a catalyst for dialogue about the adult learner and to uncover the complexities of teaching this rare and riveting species.

This book is organized around three interlocking themes: Some things we know about the adult learner; some things we know about change; and some things we know about professional development. In the process of reading the book, the reader gets a glimpse into the research that supports the theory of the adult learner, into the principles that guide the learning practices of the adult learner, and into the strategies that "work in the work setting" for the adult learner.

Chapter 1: Some Things We Know About Adult Learners

Telltale Comments

After working with adults for 20 years, we find that there are some predictable things that adult learners inevitably say. These anecdotes, based on more than cursory comments, are culled from our long experience with this unique species called the adult learner.

These telltale comments actually reveal the underlying issues and concerns of the adult learner. In fact, each of the sayings addresses a critical attribute of the adult learner's attitude that can signal the source of the fortunes and the failures of things to come for the adult teaching other adults. For that reason, each of the ten sayings is illuminated briefly in this opening discussion.

Telltale 1: "I hope this isn't a waste of my time."

Time is a priority, and adult learners want to know that the time they spend in a training, seminar, or workshop is being well spent. They want a well-organized, high-level activity that speaks to their immediate, perceived, or "recognized" need.

■ □ ■ □ ■

Case in Point

"Curves" is an exercise center that optimizes the adult's time with a pre-determined 20–30 minute routine using a pre-set equipment sequence. It's efficient, predictable, and effective.

Telltale 2: "Is this practical?"

Adults are exceptionally pragmatic about their learning. They want ideas, skills, and procedures that are readily available for their use. They want ideas that are practical, easy to use, and "ready to wear."

Case in Point

A couple planning their wedding day may take dance lessons with the specific goal of being able to dance that first dance at the wedding reception.

Telltale 3: "Can I use this right away?"

Adults learners want to take "something" back to the work setting that they can use immediately; something that helps them do their job or do their job better!

They want to put ideas into practice. So they are looking for connections from the training to the workplace. They want to know how the new learning relates to what they already do on the job.

■ □ ■ □ ■

> ## Case in Point
>
> The book, *Who Moved My Cheese?*, is about how adults embrace impending change, and is related directly to the reader's work setting.

Telltale 4: "How does this fit for me?"

Adult learners question the relevance first and the application second. They want to know how it is relevant to their situation and then they want to know how it applies to their specific circumstances.

> ## Case in Point
>
> Classroom instructional strategies for teachers need specific examples at various grade levels for relevant and easy transfer.

Telltale 5: "Who says? Who says this is better?"

This is a frequent question heard in the adult training room. Adult learners are curious about theories or research that support a given idea. They do not desire voluminous supporting research, but they do want some evidence of expert support that gives them some understanding of the "why" behind the practice. They would like some proof that the new way is not just the latest thing to come down the pike.

■☐■☐■

> ## Case in Point
>
> Participants often question what they are hearing and may even say that it is the exact opposite of what they have learned.

Telltale 6: "Show me how!"

Parallel to Telltale 5, in which the adult learner expects some substantive rationale for the innovation, is Telltale 6, in which the adult learner really wants to focus on the how. "How does one do it? How does it work? How does the process or procedure unfold?" Adults want to leave the learning activity knowing how to do it on their own. They want things modeled in real-world applications that, through demonstration, lay out the steps and illustrate the skills.

> ## Case in Point
>
> "Inspiration" software serves as a planning tool for developing mind maps, which are planning tools.

Telltale 7: "I want an expert."

Adult learners want to know that the adult teaching them knows more that they themselves know about the topic. They want a certain level of proficiency, they want stellar credentials, and they want someone who can walk the talk, not just talk the talk.

■□■□■

> ## Case in Point
>
> Proof is the popularity of a "personal trainer" for customized workout routines.

Telltale 8: "I wanna look this up on my own."

Adult learners frequently want to continue the formal lesson on their own, through research either online or through sources such as books or journals.

> ## Case in Point
>
> Taking lessons in foreign language, and supporting the work with searches about the country or the culture.

Telltale 9: "I'm here with a colleague."

Adult learners often enter into a learning setting in pairs or as a team. They come with a colleague for motivational support as well as for real support in practicing the skill. When adult learners collaborate, their confidence is boosted and their commitment to using the new information is stronger. Adult learners seem to do well in learning situations when they are accompanied by work mates and can support and coach each other.

■ □ ■ □ ■

> ## Case in Point
>
> Exercise class — go with a friend! Or for an author reading at a bookstore, go with a colleague for discussion afterward.

Telltale 10: "I already know this!"

Many times the adult learner does indeed know things about the topic or about the issue at hand. Adult learners bring a wealth of experience to the learning setting. They have rich and varied backgrounds that relate directly or indirectly to the learning, and they are constantly seeking and making connections. The connections are natural. The adult brain searches for appropriate connections to what the learner already knows. In fact, in attaching the new input to existing knowledge, adult learners activate memory and learning processes.

> ## Case in Point
>
> Accountants learning a new software package for filing taxes will find in it much of what they already know about tax law and accounting procedures and forms. It's not that new, but merely reformatted or refined.

Things We Know

At this point, readers might want to perform a short exercise. Use your prior knowledge to evaluate the 20 statements in Figure 1.1. After working through the set of statements, discuss the ideas with a colleague to see if there is a match of ideas. Then, after "due diligence," turn to the appendix, read the discussion of each of the 20 statements, and think about the implications of each.

Picturing the Adult Learner
I agree or disagree with these statements:

1. Adults seek learning experiences to cope with life-changing events.
2. For adults, learning is its own reward.
3. Adults prefer survey courses to single concept classes.
4. Adults want to use new materials.
5. Adults are quick to re-evaluate old material.
6. Adults prefer to learn alone.
7. Adults prefer to "sit and git."
8. Adults prefer "how to" trainings.
9. An eclectic approach works best with adults.
10. Non-human learning (books, TV) is popular in adult learning.
11. Adults don't like problem-centered learning.
12. Adults carry reservoirs of personal experiences.
13. "Real world" exercises are preferred.
14. Adults let their schoolwork take second seat to jobs and family.
15. Adults transfer ideas and skills easily into their work setting.
16. Adults are self-directed learners.
17. Facilitation of groups works better than lecture formats with adults.
18. Adults expect their class time to be well-spent.
19. Adult learners are voluntary, self-directed learners.
20. Adults are pragmatic learners.

Sources: Knowles, 1973; Zemke & Zemke, 1995

Figure 1.1

Adult Learning: The Research Base

Through history, the adult learner gained little attention until Malcolm Knowles focused on the adult learner population in 1973. In his seminal piece, *The Adult Learner: A Neglected Species,* Knowles drew much needed attention to what he termed the "neglected species." His premise that adult learners are an entity unto themselves speaks directly to those who teach adults. His belief that there are some fundamental facts about the adult learner that are critical to the success of programs that target this particular population has had a far-reaching impact in the field of professional learning.

As the prophecy of the information age proclaims, learning is a life-long activity. Every year, increasing numbers of adults enter formal and informal teaching/learning situations for various and sundry reasons. Although adult learners are no longer neglected in the numbers and range of programs available, the literature about adult learners is still somewhat rare. This scarcity of literature is one of the reasons this book evolved. It seems timely to publish an up-to-date synopsis of the information available about adult learners. What do we know, "in a nutshell," about this growing segment of the learning population? What are the implications for design and implementation? In brief, how might these ideas inform educator practices with adult learners?

Examining nine specific considerations sheds light on the early findings of Malcolm Knowles' writing about adult learners (Figure 1.2).

Knowles: Chart of Nine Findings from *The Adult Learner: A Neglected Species*

1. Control of their learning

2. Immediate utility

3. Focus on issues that concern them

4. Test their learning as they go

5. Anticipate how they will use their learning

6. Expect performance improvement

7. Maximize available resources

8. Require collaborative, respectful, mutual and informal climate

9. Rely on information that is appropriate and developmentally paced

Figure 1.2

Discussions of individual points present a more detailed look at each of Knowles' nine attributes of the adult learner. Interestingly, these nine findings have proven true over time and remain respected in the field as the prominent issues and concerns of the adult learner.

Point 1: Control of Their Learning

Adult learners want control of their learning. They want to decide what, where, when, and how they will learn whatever it is they have targeted for themselves. Adults want to determine the topic, the location, the timing, and the learning mode. And each of these decisions is made from an endless range of options.

Adult learners want control of their learning.

Topics: The topics range from high stakes work related skills to personal interests and leisure time pursuits.

Location: The location of the learning extends from convenient and not-so-convenient site locations to virtual learning situations, with a personal computer in the home or office.

Time Frame: Learning time encompasses full time schedules of classes and part-time schedule (nights, weekends, and summer) to anytime schedules of virtual learning.

The Mode: The mode or method of learning for adults is represented by a spectrum of choices that include face-to-face meetings at actual campuses; field-based cohort group sites; and online, video-based and Web-based models with chat rooms, Bulletin Boards, threaded discussions, and "office hours."

The choices are plentiful and the content of these choices is a given when adult learners are involved. They demand choice, as is obvious from the wealth of learning opportunities that have evolved over the years.

To further illustrate what this "control of learning" looks like, one young teacher raved about the benefits of a video-based Master's program in teaching and learning. At the top of her list of pluses was the "anytime/or my time" component because she had a new baby. She even admits that if she had had to go to a campus site for classes, she would not have been able to do her Master's at that time.

■□■□■

By contrast, one of her colleagues made a telling comment about her personal preferences when she explained that she could not imagine doing an entire Master's degree (10 courses) without substantial face-to-face time with instructors. Both consider the "control" component critical to their learning choices.

Point 2: Immediate Utility

Adult learners are clearly and unequivocally pragmatic learners. They want to know not just about the utility of what they are learning, but also about the immediacy of the utility. They want not only to use the learning, but to use it now! In essence, adults want to know just how the learning interfaces with their needs and how soon that interface will result in meaningful application.

Adults often select learning situations that have a real or an imagined sense of urgency. They have decided to take a course or attend a class or engage in some kind of instruction—for a reason. They are pursuing an interest, but that interest is in response to perceived needs.

For example, the learning may be a new exercise class called Pilates, or it may be software training in Final Cut Pro (a video-editing program). In both cases, the adult seeks not only understanding but immediate and obvious utility. The Pilates class may be needed to complete a repertoire of appropriate exercise/relaxation options, or the Final Cut Pro is needed for use on an impending video project. In either case, the adult learner senses a similar level of concern for immediate utility.

■ □ ■ □ ■

Point 3: Focus on Issues That Concern Them

Adult learners are focused learners with specific goals in mind that relate directly to their specific situations. They are quick to question the particulars that are personally relevant to them. They have almost a

Adult learners are focused learners.

tunnel vision focus, looking intently for the connections that are meaningful to them. Adult learners want to keep the focus on their own issues and are reluctant to stray off what they perceive to be the most personally relevant track. In fact, adult learners continually and persistently ask extremely focused questions that may concern only themselves. But that is their mission—to learn about the topic and how it relates to them.

A vivid and recurring example illustrates adult learners' need to focus on issues that concern them. When attending conferences or symposiums on the topic of the brain and learning, one or more adult participants invariably relate a personal story to the expert presenter (who is often a medical doctor and researcher in the field). For example, after explaining that her mother has been diagnosed with Alzheimer's Disease, the participant wants a prescriptive response from the expert. Or, another participant goes on about her mother's experience with the neurotransmitter Dopamine, and requests an appraisal or an opinion from the expert.

In both cases, the adult learner is making personal connections to the information and is focusing on related issues of concern. These adult learners are making meaning through their personally relevant examples, and they expect the expert to explicitly connect with their concerns.

Point 4: Test Their Learning as They Go

Rather than receive background theory and general information, adult learners want to test their learning along the way to mastery. They want to know how they are doing as they proceed through the learning experience! Adults want to check the mileage meter intermittently, not merely at the beginning or at the end of the journey. They want to keep their eye on the little steps, the various phases on their way to the final accomplishment. Adult learners want periodic feedback parceled out at various points along their path to mastery. They want to know how it's going. They do not want to get all the way to the end and discover that they have to learn key elements.

Adult learners want periodic feedback parceled out at various points along their path to mastery.

Adult learners are not particularly interested in background theory and general information. Rather, they want a step-by-step process that allows scaffolds to support their progress at the various stages. They want the little victories or those mini-successes along the way! Skill! Drill! Phase-by-phase, step-by-step, stage-by-stage, part-to-part, and part-to-whole.

An example of an adult learning about the computer for the first time affirms the adult learners' need to test their learning as they go. As a novice, this senior adult enlisted the services of a computer coach to get familiar with the new-fangled machine. As the learner progressed during several days of coaching, he insisted on "little performances along the way."

■ □ ■ □ ■

From the simple task of turning on the computer to the more complex tasks of activating e-mail and searching the Web for medical information, this senior citizen insisted on stopping to demonstrate mastery of each piece! Although the coach understood the hesitancy of the adult learner to forge forward on the more complex operations, she had not realized the need for testing simpler bits of information. Yet, it illustrates the real concerns of adults as learners. They want to know they know, before they get too far along.

Point 5: Anticipate How They Will Use Their Learning

Closely related to the Point 2 concerns of "immediate utility," Point 5 says that adults scan their cognition horizons for ways to apply their learning. Often, throughout the entire time they are learning something, adult learners are eagerly anticipating ways to use the new ideas. They look for ways to slot the learning into their own personal lives.

Adults have clear and definite expectations for transfer. They are pragmatically poised for relevant and meaningful opportunities to use the new information. In fact, it is in these natural expectations for transfer that adult learners separate themselves from the younger set. Children may learn mostly for the sake of learning, but adults seem programmed to learn for purposeful utility.

Adults are pragmatically poised for relevant and meaningful opportunities to use the new information.

One example of anticipating how they will use their learning manifests itself when

■ □ ■ □ ■

adults learn a foreign language. If they are taking Spanish classes, it is often related to an upcoming trip to a Spanish-speaking country. While adults are working hard to learn the language, they are busy anticipating when they will actually be using it. This focused anticipation is evidenced by adults who ask the instructor how to say "vineyard" in Spanish because they are planning to visit the wine country, or how to say, "bullfight" because that is a stop on their itinerary. Although it sounds almost silly to talk about anticipated application, because all learning is for transfer, it really is a hallmark of adult learning.

Anticipated application is a hallmark of adult learning.

Point 6: Expect Performance Improvement

Parallel to several other concerns mentioned previously, adult learners expect to see their performance improved as a result of their classes or lessons. Adults sign up for a skiing lesson, specifically to develop and/or hone a particular skill, such as skiing the moguls, and they expect to "be better" after having taken the lesson.

Adults bring varying levels of skill and expertise to the learning, and they are continually self-appraising as they learn. They expect noticeable improvements and are not shy about saying so. In fact, when adults do not see the progress they are expecting, they are quick to evaluate the instructor as ineffective or unskilled as a teacher. They reason that they are willing and capable students who have volunteered for the classes. If they are not showing marked improvement,

Adults are continually self-appraising as they learn.

surely the fault must be the instructor's, not theirs—after all, they are motivated learners.

An example similar to the skiing illustration is that of the adult learners who sign up for private golf lessons. They are willing participants in an analysis of their grip, their stance, and their swing, with the full expectation that they will see a notable difference in their execution of the golf swing. If they don't, adult learners have been known to gripe and complain about the lesson, the instructor, the equipment, the time of day, the time of year, the weather, the lack of weather, etc. You get the picture. They expected real improvement, and they were not seeing it.

Point 7: Maximize Available Resources

To maximize available resources, teachers working with adults take advantage of the vast experience and resources that adults bring to the learning. These knowing teachers tap into the wealth of materials adult learners have access to. They willingly and assertively connect to the generosity of sprit of the adult learners who eagerly share their personal vault of tried-and-true resources. The most effective teachers of adult learners maximize all available resources with photocopies, annotated bibliographies, Web-site addresses, and any other means that make these resources available and accessible to all. This relentless tendency to gather and share creates the richness and depth often found in adult learners. In brief, the wise teacher honors the expertise of the adult learner.

The most effective teachers of adult learners maximize all available resources.

A perfect example of how to maximize resources for effective adult learning is captured in the graduate education class on data-driven decisions. As soon as the topic becomes "ways to manage the data," participants flood the discussion with every kind of data management software known to man. They share a lengthy litany of experiences with various and sundry software programs and hardware companies. By making this readily available to the adult learners in the class, everyone benefits. Each adult in the room can zero in on the management system that fits his or her situation. The sharing of resources illuminates the entire discussion and enlightens the issues for various adult learners.

Point 8: Require Collaborative, Respectful, Mutual, and Informal Climate

Adult learners want to collaborate and share. They thrive on the back-and-forth exchange of ideas and the negotiated issues that emerge. Adults are social creatures. They have honed their social skills and are skilled team members. They understand the power of dialogue and seek advice and commentary from their colleagues. Adult learners know the value of a "reasoned opinion," and they have a genuine respect for the thoughts and reactions from their peers. In addition, adults embrace the ideas of mutual respect and mutual learning situations that are both somewhat unstructured and informal. They relish the give-and-take of mutually beneficial dialogues and the seesaw of complementary or opposing ideas. Adult learners seek social settings and are stimulated through discussion and articulation of ideas.

Adults are social creatures.

To exemplify this need for a respectful and social climate of informality and mutual benefits, just think for a moment about the most stimulating seminar you ever took. Think about how exciting it was to have rigorous arguments that exposed different views and sparked further debate and, eventually, deep insight into the issues. This is one example of the collaborative spirit that drives the adult learner.

Point 9: Rely on Information That Is Appropriate and Developmentally Paced

Adult learners want the learning paced developmentally, without great gaps or giant leaps to remotely connected information or information that goes beyond their comfort zones. They will even say, "I don't want to know about that, yet! I just need to concentrate on this part. After I get this conquered, I'll think about the next thing. I can only handle this right now. Don't give me too much, too soon. It doesn't compute."

Adult learners know when they do not know. They are more metacognitive about their learning than young learners. Adults are aware of their own understanding and prefer to move gingerly to the next step. Adults pace themselves, and they will pace their learning even when the instructor does not honor their need for developmentally appropriate phases. As soon as a "leap" is sensed, they back up and almost demand a more logical and incremental path.

Adults pace their learning.

An example that comes to mind is of two couples learning to play bridge. One of the four is an expert bridge player and has taken on the task of teaching the

■ □ ■ □ ■

other three. The three adults learning about bridge come to the table with various levels of understanding and actual experience with the game itself. As the instruction progresses, the expert tries to move from the fundamentals of arranging the hand and counting points to the concept of a game, a partial game, and a rubber. As soon as he starts to describe these elements of scoring, all three adult learners protest. They are focused on counting their points and trying to determine appropriate bids based on their hands. They are not able to shift focus and consider the bid in reference to winning a game or rubber. They simply are not there, yet. Developmentally, they are not ready to tackle anything else. They want to succeed at this bidding stage, first.

Five Assumptions About Adult Learners

In his seminal text, *The Adult Learner: A Neglected Species* (1973), Malcolm Knowles presents a comprehensive adult learning theory. He uses the term *androgogy*, coined by Kapp in 1833 and developed by Lindeman (1926), to describe "the art and science of helping adults learn." For Knowles, androgogy takes on a broader meaning, one that refers to "learner-focused education for all ages." Knowles believes that andragogy is process-oriented rather than content-based (pedagogy). He anchors his theory on five main assumptions as depicted in Figure 1.3.

■ □ ■ □ ■

Five Assumptions About Adult Learners

1. Self-concept: The adult learner moves toward being a self-directed human being.

2. Experience: The adult learner accumulates a personal growing reservoir of experiences.

3. Readiness to Learn: The adult learner is oriented to developmental tasks of social roles.

4. Orientation to Learning: The adult learner is problem-centered and aware of the immediacy of application.

5. Motivation: The adult learner harbors internal motivation.

Figure 1.3

Self-Concept of the Adult Learner

Adult learners are directing their own plan.

The self-concept of adult learners focuses on a move away from a dependent personality toward being a self-directed human being. Adult learners are directing their own plan. They schedule learning into busy calendars, and they do their own diagnosing and prescribing about learning opportunities they need and about what learning experiences they will embrace. Adult learners are, in effect, driven by their individual concepts of self.

Experience of the Adult Learner

Adult learners bring much to the table.

As people mature, they are constantly and continually adding to their expanding repertoire of experiences. This phenomenon of an ever-growing reservoir of knowledge provides an increasing resource for learning. Adult learners bring much to the table. The traditional concept of "tabula rasa," or blank slate, in no way applies to the adult learner. Rather, adult learners have a rich and extensive bank of experiences to draw from.

Adult Learners Readiness to Learn

Adults' readiness to learn is anchored to developmental tasks that are necessary for their social roles, whether at home, at work or in the community. In other words, adults are focused and ready in a highly pragmatic way. They are eager to learn skills, concepts, and attitudes that are obviously and directly related to their work, their families, or themselves. They want to learn those things that make their lives easier or better in some substantive way. They are often ready, willing, and able to learn. In fact, they are so focused on application that the phrase, "Ready! Fire! Aim!" sometimes applies, rather than the standard Ready! Aim! Fire! sequence.

Adults are focused and ready in a highly pragmatic way.

Adult Learners Orientation to Learn

As suggested previously, adult learners' perspective is not one of a postponed application that may seem obscure and remote but rather one of immediacy of application and use. They are poised to use the new learning in real problem-centered ways. In fact, they expect to apply their learning at once, to fulfill a need or to address an issue they have. Again, adult

Adult learners are highly oriented to learning for an immediate purpose or impending concern.

■ □ ■ □ ■

learners are highly oriented to learning for an immediate purpose or impending concern.

Adult Learners' Motivation to Learn

Adult learners have intrinsic motivation to learn. They are self-directed eager learners or "omnivores" who devour everything and anything connected to their goals. They cannot get enough, fast enough to make them happy. Adult learners are learning for a reason, and they push themselves from within. They are sparked by an inner source and have a sense of urgency about their learning.

Adult learners cannot get enough, fast enough to make them happy.

Knowle's work is considered seminal still. His classic book on adult learners has been revised and updated as *The Adult Learner: The Definitive Classic in Adult Education and Human Resource Development* (1998). While preserving the best of Knowle's previous edition, Holton and Swanson incorporate the latest developments in adult learning theory and practice.

Supporting Assumptions About Adult Learners

Complementary studies reveal a list of assumptions similar to those of Knowles that support a parallel view. Dirkx, Lavin, and Pelavin (1995) state that experts generally agree on the four assumptions listed in Figure 1.4.

■ □ ■ □ ■

Four Supporting Assumptions About Adult Learners

1. Diverse, active learners
2. Problem-oriented
3. Control their own learning
4. Strong sense of self

Figure 1.4

Diverse, Active Learners

Adult learners are diverse learners; they bring a wealth of life experiences to their learning activity; and they vary widely in age, abilities, level of schooling, job experiences, cultural background, and personal goals, Yet, all carry a reservoir of personal experiences that serve them well in new learning situations.

Adult Learners Are Problem-Oriented

Adult learners want to relate their learning to specific contexts in their lives, ones that usually involve work, their homes and families, or their avocations. They tend to be pragmatic learners, seeking to improve their performance, yet schoolwork takes a back seat to other responsibilities. Because they are busy people with many items on their plates, adult learners expect their class time to be well spent and anticipate that their course will help them with existing problem areas.

Adult learners expect their class time to be well spent.

Control Over Their Own Learning

Adult learners tend to be voluntary learners who take seriously their decision to return to school. They believe that education will be helpful, and they want to exercise some degree of control over their learning. Their maturity level and familiarity with the content often determines a greater or lesser degree of self-directedness.

Adult learners want to exercise some degree of control over their learning.

Strong Sense of Self

Adult learners, naturally, have varying degrees of self-efficacy; yet, for the most part, they demonstrate a strong sense of self in their learning. Even so, some feel embarrassed about returning to school or joining classes of younger students. Some may hold negative impressions of their own abilities, or they may hold negative impressions of schools, teachers, and educational experiences in general. They may have varying level of awareness about their own learning styles. Yet, adult learners sense of self does have significant influence on the meaning of the learning situation and their sense of accomplishment. In sum, the adult learner's sense of self greatly influences their learning experiences.

Adult learners demonstrate a strong sense of self in their learning.

Notice the close relationships between the Knowles assumptions about adult learners in the early studies and Dirkx, Lavin, and Pelavin's 1995 study.

■□■□■

Krupp's Work on Adult Learners

Another pioneer in this field of adult learning was Judy Erin Krupp, whose work on adult learners is heralded through her affiliation with the National Staff Development Council. Although her work (Krupp, 1981, 1982) was abruptly halted by her untimely death, her insight into the ages and phases of adult learners, although far too comprehensive to include here, are classic pieces to study if you are involved with adult learners.

Yet, even with the advantage of the knowledge of these experts, the field of study about adult learners is still somewhat barren ground, with dribbles of information emerging all the time. It is definitely fertile territory for further research and writings.

Thirty Things We Know for Sure

Zemke and Zemke (1995) present a comprehensive summary on "some things we know for sure about the adult learner" in their classic article that appeared in the 1990s. A glance at their article, *Thirty Things We Know for Sure*, reveals three categorical areas in which the authors present a cogent view of the adult learner. The categories include motivation to learn, curriculum design, and classroom instructional designs.

Three elements emerge in the section on motivation: preference for real-world, problem-based approaches; the opportunity for personal growth or gain; and the role of increased participation in motivating the adult learner.

■□■□■

In the area of curricular design, Zemke and Zemke identify eight areas of concern:

1. Problem-centered curriculum models

2. The need for pre-assessments

3. Integration of information

4. Fidelity in case studies and exercises

5. Feedback and recognition

6. Accommodation of various learning styles

7. Accommodation of adults continued growth and changing values

8. The need for transfer strategies.

Although all eight are addressed in the section on curriculum, some of the ideas overlap with their discussion about "In the Classroom," which addresses the ideas of a safe learning environment, the preference for facilitation rather than lecture mode, and methods and techniques for promoting understanding and fostering transfer.

■□■□■

Chapter 2: Some Things We Know About Change

The idea that staff developers and other leadership in the school are in the role of change agents is not new. In fact, Fullan (1982) writes extensively about educational change over the years, as does Sarason (1982) and Hargreaves (1994). In addition, Guskey (2000) adds to this field of literature in his work on change theory and the role of professional development. All agree on one overriding premise: Change is not easy. To bring about meaningful change takes time, energy, and patience, accompanied by a well-articulated plan that stretches over time. Adult learners change slowly. They are ingrained in their ways, and they do not abandon their comfort zone easily.

Change is not easy.

This Horse Is Not Dead

As educators think about an event or time of change such as a science textbook adoption, a move from a junior high school model to a middle school concept, or a shift from the high school bell schedule to a more flexible block schedule, the resisting statements abound.

Several tools serve as catalysts for discussion and insight into the idea of the reluctance of adult learners to change. One of these powerful tools appears as a poem of sorts, called, *This Horse Is Not Dead!* Figure 2.1 shows 12 humorous statements adult learners could easily say when faced with the fear of substantive and meaningful change. Listen, and you will hear the creative reluctance that is all too common in the teachers' lounge or in the office meeting. In examining these comments, there is the definite ring of truth, albeit with a touch of humor.

This Horse Is Not Dead

1. Buy a stronger whip.

2. Change riders.

3. Say, "This is the way we have always done it."

4. Appoint a committee.

5. Visit other sites.

6. Increase standards to ride a dead horse.

7. Appoint a team.

8. Create a training session.

9. Change requirements, declaring "This horse is not dead."

10. Hire a consultant.

11. Do a cost analysis.

12. Promote horse to a supervisory position.

Figure 2.1

To demonstrate this, the anecdote uses the metaphor of "switching horses." The first thing they say is, "This horse is not dead! He's already broken in and has a lot of life left." This reluctance is coded in teacher-talk as "I have all my lesson plans done for this!" Others say, "Buy a stronger whip, or, "Change riders;" in education code, this stands for the staff are not using the horse the right way, and they need more supervision or maybe even new staff members. Still other resistors are heard to lament with the age-old excuse, "We have always done it this way, before."

Some are more creative in their resistance and are full of fertile suggestions: "Appoint a committee or a team to study the problem!" or better yet, "Let's visit some other sites and see what they are doing." Others take a more aggressive stance with their resistance and ask for either an increase in the standards or a change in the requirements, announcing that, "This horse is not dead."

Still others protest that more vigorous action is needed and put a positive spin on their reluctance to change: "Let's do a cost analysis, hire a consultant, and create a training session to help us." And, finally, the ultimate solution reveals itself, when the protesters suggest, with a straight face and a earnest tone, "Let's promote the horse to a supervisory position."

These are real comments heard from adult resisters. They are both funny and sad. When put in the context of "This horse is not dead" and "There is no need to change horses," they are hilarious. Yet, when put in the context of changing to an up-to-date and improved science text, facilitating a move to a middle school concept for increased self-esteem and academic achievement of the adolescent, or scheduling by blocks of time in the high school schedule for more authentic learning, then these excuses ring shallow and false.

(To have a little fun with this idea of how vehemently adults resist change, leaders can look for a picture book version of these statements that is delightful to read at a team meeting or a faculty gathering. Share *If You're Riding a Horse and It Dies, Get Off,* by Grant and Forsten (1999) and enjoy the raucous discussion that ensues.)

■ □ ■ □ ■

Here is a story that illustrates the depth of resistance adults harbor, knowingly or unknowingly. After some faculty members recommended her as an author and expert in the areas of curriculum integration, a staff development consultant was hired by their principal to work with the school's staff as they created an interdisciplinary curriculum for students in an alternative degree program. As the principal explained the plan, all the teachers seemed very positive and ready, willing, and able to move in the direction of their goals. Yet, they had been working with this concept of integrating the curriculum for more than two years and not one integrated unit had ever been implemented by any one on the faculty. As the consultant began working with the group, the problem started to become obvious. The two teachers who, as the co-chairs of the committee to integrate curriculum, were supposed to lead the integration effort were, in reality, blocking the team. Each step of the way, at every turn, they would scrutinize the input to the point that they stopped all forward progress. They questioned, endlessly, the appropriateness of every proposed theme; they deliberated about the time frame for teaching the themes; they wondered about the size and make up of the interdisciplinary teams.Of course, because they were the leaders, others followed their lead. As the two continually posed thoughtful questions about the various elements, others took their objections to heart. Consequently, the group never really made definite decisions about anything. They always left things "on the table" for further discussion. Well-intentioned as they were, the two leaders were too tentative about the actual implementation. Their fear of the unknown prevailed; their ability to accept the ideas, even if imperfect, to move the

The fear of change has great power over the adult learner.

■ □ ■ □ ■

project along was effectively stymied. The fear of change has great power over the adult learner.

The Change Game

Guskey (2000) presents a case for change in schools through professional development. Yet, the change process he describes may be quite different from the way most people think change happens. To explore the idea of the change process, readers may want to try a simple exercise. Write the four elements in Figure 2.2 on four separate cards or sticky notes.

Elements of the Change Process

Professional Development

Change in Practice

Change in Student Achievement

Change in Belief

Figure 2.2

Now, move the cards into the appropriate left to right sequence to represent how you think change occurs through professional development. If possible, share your thinking with someone else. Next, read what Guskey (2000) says about this complex and elusive process called change.

■□■□■

Guskey relates that most people think change following a professional development experience occurs like this: First, participants go to professional development; next, participants change their beliefs about the idea; then, they see changes in student achievement; and finally, they change their practice.

Yet, Guskey believes that the real sequence is this: Professional development occurs; teachers change their practice by trying something in their classrooms; they see student achievement increase; and, eventually, they begin to change their belief systems. He claims that teachers change their belief systems only after, not before, they see evidence of some positive change. And, he thinks that, even then, change in belief systems occurs over time. It is usually not a sudden "Aha!" moment.

> **Teachers change their belief systems only after, not before, they see evidence of some positive change.**

A real example of initiating the idea of cooperative learning illustrates this process. Following Guskey's model, teachers receive professional development in the structures and strategies of cooperative learning groups. They then go back to their classrooms and change their direct instruction practices by adding a cooperative learning task to the lesson. They notice interesting changes in the achievement of some students: Kids who never offer a response, talk in their groups; others take active, leadership roles for their assigned responsibility as part of the team; still others show evidence of understanding the information in authentic ways. As the teachers note these positive signs of learning, they begin to question their long-held beliefs that kids learn best through

> **Change in belief systems takes many trials and encompasses many tribulations as well as much time and energy.**

a direct instruction approach. Slowly, over time, as these teachers continue to read and learn about cooperative learning, they gradually shift their beliefs. And, eventually, they institutionalize the change by making cooperative learning a critical component of every lesson. But, this change in belief systems takes many trials and encompasses many tribulations as well as much time and energy. Change, real change in one's beliefs, is just not very easy.

In fact, even after many years of working with cooperative learning, teachers quietly confess that they still think they should be in front of the class "teaching." That is their picture of what teaching is...and it's so hard to alter that view. Although this idea of change through professional development is revisited in the next section, it is notable to understand at this point that change occurs first through changing practices, then through changing beliefs.

Change occurs first through changing practices, then through changing beliefs.

Who Moved My Cheese?

Spencer Johnson offers another view of change through his groundbreaking book, *Who Moved My Cheese?* (1998). In this delightful allegory, there are four memorable characters who illustrate how different people approach change with very different attitudes and very different actions. In the story, there are two mice, Sniff and Scurry, and two little human beings, Hem and Haw. Each reacts differently as he discovers that the cheese that has always been in exactly the same place has, suddenly and without explanation, disappeared. Thus, the question each asks is, naturally, "Who moved my cheese?"

■ □ ■ □ ■

Notice the different paths they take as they deal with the idea of change as symbolized by the cheese that has been moved. Sniff, the first little mouse, sniffs out the change early and is one of the first to acknowledge its movement and talk about possibilities. Scurry, the second little mouse, scurries into action immediately and starts hunting for the cheese. Then, of course, there's Hem, one of the little people, who hems and haws relentlessly about the missing cheese, hangs around, and in the end, never totally accepts the change. That leaves Haw, who hangs around long enough to embrace the change, even if a bit reluctantly. Haw is laughing, "Haw, haw, haw, the last laugh is on me, because I did, finally, find the cheese. I did finally, accept the change, even if I was kicking and screaming all the way."

Although this story is just an allegory about how people react to change, it offers a wonderful platform for further thinking about change. In fact, readers may want to get their own copy of the book and read the story in its entirety as they track their own reactions to change. They may be surprised and recognize themselves as one of the four imaginary characters.

To illustrate how powerfully accurate this allegory portrays people in the change process, there is a parallel story that really happened to some real people. It is the story of a small publishing company that was purchased by a large publishing company. As the merger was happening, one employee (Sniff) sniffed out the change early and began positioning himself for a positive role in the transition. Another employee (Scurry) scurried into action and chose to leave the company shortly after the merger. A third employee (Hem) blundered around, never really embracing the merger, yet hanging on to his position for the security of it. Hem was on board in name only and was not at all happy with the new company. In fact, he complained, resisted, and often took on the role of devil's advocate in company decision-making efforts. A fourth employee (Haw), on the other hand, did stay long enough to accept the inevitable changes and joined the team wholeheartedly. Haw, as it turns out, became a valued employee to the merged company as a needed resource, because he could add insight to decisions through his historical knowledge of the former company.

Each, in very different ways, managed the change. Most accepted the change, from the small, family-owned "Mom and Pop" shop to the rewards and demands of a large, corporate publishing firm. Some preferred to "jump ship" and seek employment in other venues. Yet, each did what was comfortable and, probably, right to satisfy individual wants and needs.

So, the lesson seems to be that a change agent must honor each and every reaction to change, as those in the change process are reacting the only way they know how. The change agent must remember that people involved in the change are doing the best they can. Some come along quickly and easily, others more slowly. And, some do not come along at all. That is just the way it is.

The best advice for the change agent is, perhaps, to go with the ones who are ready. Do not worry too much about the others. Do not let the reluctant ones become a drain on the entire process and zap the energy from the project. Allow them to find their comfort zone and work with them in the best ways possible

> **The best advice for the change agent is, perhaps, to go with the ones who are ready.**

■ ☐ ■ ☐ ■

Group Process: Roles People Play

A graduate student in education recalls the major impact on him of the classic text by Schmuck and Schmuck, (1997), *Group Processes in the Classroom*, in which the authors present revealing discussions about the various roles that learners play as they participate and become accepted and contributing members of various small groups. These roles seem to apply to the adult learner as well.

To examine the idea of small groups a bit more closely, consider the number and kinds of formal and informal small groups that adults are involved with: the bridge club, the golf foursome, the car pool, the exercise class at Curves, the Cubs Fan Club, the poker game guys, the volleyball team, the dog show people, and family events. These are just a few examples of the little gatherings that adult learners attend and participate in regularly.

Adults also often interact with more formal small groups: school boards, faculty meetings, Parent Teacher Associations, community committees, department/grade level meetings, corporate seminars, graduations, award ceremonies, legal proceedings, and various and sundry institutional kinds of meetings and conferences.

As the adult learners immerse themselves in these intellectual and social activities, they tend to take on specific and definitive roles in the group. Each becomes known for the role(s) that comes to them so naturally. Someone usually takes on the role of caretaker or nurturer, another assumes the role of the devil's advocate or blocker, and still another plays the role of the sage or know-it-all.

Some of these roles are helpful and necessary to move the group forward, whereas others, most likely to be considered the negative roles, tend to consume time and negate any real progress. Yet, for whatever reason, these seemingly unhelpful roles frequently emerge as part of the small group process. Regardless of the circumstance, many of these roles can be recognized in small group settings. In fact, if one of the members leaves the group, either permanently or temporarily, someone else steps in to take over the absented role.

Adult learners tend to take on specific and definitive roles in the group.

In a subsequent discussion, various roles that have been observed and documented by the authors and by the experts are described and delineated in some detail (Figure 2.3). It is suggested that, as readers read the discussion, they mentally try to slot the roles into their own real-world situations. It is expected that any adult reading this piece will have a sense of déjà vu, as they encounter myriad personalities and match them to their own lives. In addition, the exercise provides incredible insights into the dynamics of small groups interactions, reactions, and eventual actions.

■□■□■

Cast of Characters

1. Caretaker

2. Know-it-all

3. Hitchhiker

4. Blocker (Devil's Advocate)

5. Omnivore

6. Inquisitor

7. Negotiator

8. Over-Achiever

9. Parliamentarian

10. Sage

11. The Clown

Figure 2.3

Caretaker

Naturally, the caretaker role involves the nurturing and looking after of the others in the group. The caretaker, concerned about the creature comforts for the group, checks the temperature of the team with queries such as, "Do we need a little break?" "Is it time to wrap this up and continue when we are fresh? Or, Is everyone comfortable with this agenda, schedule or decisions?" The caretaker has a vital role in the group's wellness, which spontaneously affects the productivity and, subsequently, the outcomes of the group. This is Florence Nightingale, reincarnated. This is the ultimate nurse, at her best.

Know-It-All

This is the role of the pseudo-expert, not the role of the authentic sage. The know-it-all has a telling comment for every idea and is more than willing to share it. This role player can monopolize the group and absorb gobs of time because he or she feels obliged to share every scrap of information with the group. When this role player is discovered and recognized for what he or she is, others tend to tune out as soon as the rhetoric starts. The group closes its ears to the incessant preaching and pontificating. This is a difficult role for facilitators to handle and requires skill and finesse.

Hitchhiker

The hitchhiker is just that, someone who wants and accepts a free ride. The hitchhiker is just along for the ride and often contributes little or nothing to the group. Consequently, the group soon knows not to look his or her way for any substantive contributions, leaving the hitchhiker to become a silent passenger in the "vehicle." The hitchhiker is often a passive learner and a docile thinker who appears fairly removed from the action. He or she seems to take this role regardless of the group. More often than not, it seems to be part of this learner's demeanor.

Blocker (Devil's Advocate)

The blocker role is sometimes referred to in small groups as the devil's advocate. This person tends to take contrary positions in the discussion and frequently apologizes for the interruption, but insists that he or she has a cogent point that needs to be voiced. More often than not, these insertions tend to sideline the main discussion and may even cause untimely delays in the meeting agenda. Yet, there are times when the devil's advocate, rather than blocking the decision, brings up an important point that leads to a needed compromise that gets everyone on board with the final stance.

Omnivore

Bruce Joyce and Beverly Showers (1995) often refer to the motivated adult learner as the "omnivore"—the one who devours everything and is not satisfied until he or she knows every last detail of the issues at hand. The omnivore is the highly motivated eager beaver of the group, often pursuing a point beyond the interest of others. Yet, this is an example of the adult learner who is often a pleasure to work with because she pushes the leader to be more comprehensive about some things.

Inquisitor

The inquisitor not only asks questions constantly, but also sometimes acts more like a player in the "inquisition." Some questions are relevant and to the point, while others are over the top and way beyond the point. The inquisitor asks such things as this: "How many?" "How much?" "When and Where?" "What's the time line for this?" "How many of us want to make this commitment?" "Is there a better plan that we haven't thought of, yet?" "How does this compare to last year?" Although some of these questions actually hit on authentic questions harbored by other members of a "silent majority" in the group, some are rather meaningless to many of the others in the group.

■□■□■

Negotiator

There is always a negotiator who takes on the role of bargaining for the group. This is the persistent person who negotiates meeting times, a lesser amount of work due, the location of the next meeting, or even the length of a lunch break. This is the "professional negotiator" who knows just when and how to word the request so that the leader(s) must stop everything and show thoughtful consideration to the "reasonable" request. However, these requests often are out of context to what is going on at the moment and tend to create sidebars to the action at hand. (Note: a perfect corollary to this discussion on the "cast of characters" is the children's book, by Doreen Cronin, called *Click, Clack, Moo*. In this delightful tale of farm animals, the role of negotiation is made crystal clear. Although an illustrated picture book for younger readers, its subtle message is almost more appropriate for adult learners.)

Over-Achiever

The over-achiever is similar to but different from the omnivore. Although both are motivated learners, the focus for the omnivore is during the input stage of getting information, while the focus for the over-achiever is in output stage of giving information. The over-achiever goes into full swing when the assignments are due. He or she puts tremendous effort into the assigned tasks and goes above and beyond the call of duty in submitting comprehensive and superior products. The over-achiever feels a sense of accomplishment as he or she individually tackles a piece of the puzzle for the group.

Parliamentarian

The parliamentarian keeps the group on track with his or her frequent "calls to order." This role embraces the activities of the "policy police," as the role player insists on "law and order" or at least *Robert's Rules of Order.* The parliamentarian demands a faithful following of the procedures of order—the rules and regulations and the acknowledged forms and norms set and accepted by the group. He or she is as interested in the process as in the progress or the product. This person is in it for the journey, not merely the destination. Some things they say include: "Didn't we agree to vote after all the ideas have been fully explained?" "Haven't we extended our rule about time limits for members to present their case?" "I'd like to propose that we review the procedure we agreed to last time."

Sage

The sage is the master/mentor of the group. This person garners the role for him- or herself, or, more likely, the team benevolently bestows the role of sage on that deserving soul. The sage has formal and informal power in the group. He or she can control the flow simply by withholding opinions or by not giving the informal nod of agreement or look of consensus. In a more formal action, the sage can approve or disapprove an idea with or without justification. The sage, by the nature of the role, holds an enormous amount of power. Sages may be seasoned and experienced members of the group, or they may be the person who is most qualified, is certified, or holds the highest degree or title. Again, this is a role that greatly influences the work of the group. The sage, many times and in many cases, has the last word.

The Clown

Although the role of clown may seem like a frivolous one or one that groups can do without, this role is actually critical to the success of an ongoing group. The clown brings levity to the scene and, in many situations, supplies the needed humor to diffuse a mounting conflict between members of the group. The clown understands when the group is immersed in a "sticky wicket situation" and skillfully provides a timely remark or a telling wisecrack that frequently brings emotions back to a more neutral level. In fact, the group counts on the clown to monitor tight situations and to intercede when emotions get too high or when anger, sarcasm, and cynicism begin to seep into the group's process. The clown acts almost like an informal referee or umpire, checking the tenor of the group and interceding when necessary. Of course, the clown can overplay the role and grind on people's nerves, yet, in the end, humor is great medicine for any team.

If readers have not already been recognizing the various roles that are evident in the groups they belong to, it is a useful exercise to apply these ideas by reviewing the list and trying a few of the most obvious labels on a few participants. It is also recommended by the authors that the "cast of characters" be discussed within groups. Just the awareness of these roles offers insights and discoveries about the group and how it does its best work.

■ □ ■ □ ■

The Three-Tier Change Process

When readers explore the work of Michael Fullan (1991), who has been writing about the "meaning of educational change" for more than 30 years, they are visiting the concept of the change process. Guskey's model, addressed previously in the text, also explores this phenomenon. Fullan's writings are basic in the study of change and offer a comprehensive model for facilitating the change process, particularly in schools. A professor at the University of Toronto and a charter member of the Ontario Institute for the Study of Education, Fullan offers a simple model for understanding the complex process of change. In addition, he speaks and writes about what does and does not work as schools and institutions attempt to bring about meaningful change.

Fullan offers a simple model for understanding the complex process of change.

One of Fullan's most seminal contributions is a three-tier process for understanding how change occurs. The three stages are simple: Stage 1, Initiate the innovation; Stage 2, Implement the innovation, and Stage 3, Institutionalize the innovation (Figure 2.4).

Three-Tier Change Process

Stage 1: Initiate the change — Introduce the innovation to the participants.

Stage 2: Implement the change — Apply the tools and techniques of the innovation.

Stage 3: Institutionalize the change — Establish accountability for continued use.

Figure 2.4

Sounds simple enough. Initiate, implement, and institutionalize. Let's take a more detailed look at each of the three stages.

Stage 1: Initiate

First, to initiate the innovation means to plan an introductory awareness that establishes the context, the goals, the process, and the timeline for all who are involved. It means bringing in the big guns or developing a video or a powerful multimedia presentation. Initiation calls for inclusion of all stakeholders and invites them to participate, to question, to acknowledge their concerns and, eventually, to announce their level of commitment to the change.

Initiation calls for incluion of all stakeholders.

In understanding this earliest stage of the change process, it is important to notice that there needs to be an energizing level of excitement. Some participants will anticipate the best possible scenario, others, the worst-case scenario. Some are eager to see the plan unfold; others dread the effort it will take. Some cannot wait for the innovation to begin; others cannot wait until it is over. Yet, for both the one who anticipates and the who dreads the innovation, this initiation stage signals all concerned that things are going to be changing.

Stage 2: Implement

To implement the innovation takes on another meaning entirely. This is the stage when the plan is put into practice. During the implementation stage, the change is applied in real and meaningful ways. Models are

This is the stage when the plan is put into practice.

introduced through sustained, job-embedded professional development that announces the innovation with integrity and the needed input to support the change. It is in this stage that attention is given to the appropriate practice, feedback, and coaching needed to ensure success. In short, this is when the "proof is in the pudding"; when the participants must move past the "talk the talk" phase to the "walk the talk" phase; and when the rubber hits the road. The innovation moves from theory to practice.

Stage 3: Institutionalize

To institutionalize the change means that the initial innovation permeates every aspect of the institution and becomes ingrained in the very principles, practices, and policies of the institution. Everyone knows that these innovations have become integral to the overall expectations of all who are involved with the institution. They accept no excuses. This is the way things are done, and everyone is expected to comply.

> **To institutionalize an idea is usually a long and enduring journey with stops and starts along the way.**

Of course, to institutionalize an innovation requires persistence and patience. It takes time, rehearsal, repetition, and practice for participants in the innovation to move from novice levels to competent and proficient levels of performance. It takes financial, emotional, and professional support to adopt an innovation of such magnitude that it is the essence of the institution. To institutionalize an idea is usually a long and enduring journey with stops and starts along the way. It is a journey of obstacles and challenges, of readiness and rewards, of faith and fellowship. And, when levels of achievement are realized along the way, when there is some level of satisfaction for all concerned, it is a journey that dictates genuine celebrations. These are the celebrations that articulate the well-deserved success of the change process.

This brief introduction to the change process is simply a testing of the waters. As suspected, it is much more complex than described here.

In fact, although the process sounds so simple, even Fullan (1991) cautions that there are many concerns to be aware of. One early concern is that initiating the innovation frequently can take over the entire process of change. When the initiation process goes overboard, when it becomes too comprehensive, too complicated, and too complex, participants become overwhelmed. They become worn out in this first stage, a stage that can inadvertently go on for weeks, months, and even years. By the time the implementation stage begins, people are burned out, negative, and resistant to do anything more.

> **One early concern is that initiating the innovation frequently can take over the entire process of change.**

This is just one of the many obstacles that interfere with the change process. Be wary. If new to examining and understanding the process of change, take time to investigate this concept more deeply. Readings by Fullan, Hargreaves, Guskey, Little, and Gregory are recommended references.

Looking at Fullan's Change Process

Usually, to illustrate the three phases of the change process as described by Fullan, one would look at the change process at a single school or district for making a particular innovation. However, sometimes, one part of the change process for a single innovation works smoothly and is really a fine example for discussion, while other parts of that process may have issues about effectiveness. For that

■□■□■

reason, in this discussion, each phase is illuminated by the actions at a school or district that presents the change most effectively. The three examples selected are exemplary models of a particular phase of the change process.

Example: Initiating the Innovation for Change

When a New Mexico school district planned the change to a seventh and eighth grade junior high building, they decided they would try to incorporate some of the middle school concepts in order to ensure as smooth a transition as possible for the early adolescents involved in the change. That decision lead to other discussions about what the middle school concept was all about and about how to get information about the concept to the various stakeholders. One idea for introducing the middle school concept was to hold a town meeting of sorts, on a Saturday. Invitations were sent to about 50 people, including board members, principals, teachers, students, parents, and community leaders. An expert in middle level education facilitated the session, as participants became familiar with the elements involved in the middle school concept.

One idea for introducing the middle school concept was to hold a town meeting of sorts, on a Saturday.

As a beginning step for initiating the change from a departmentalized junior high to a more blended model of middle school elements, this town meeting strategy had a positive impact with those involved. The initiation plan included follow-up meetings using members of the original group as facilitation teams. This plan got the change process off the ground and on its way toward implementation.

■□■□■

Example: Implementing the Innovation for Change

The staff at an Illinois school not only was planning its transition from a traditional bell schedule to a more robust block schedule model but also was in the midst of a building expansion project. As they talked about the impact of the block schedule on instructional designs, each department had opportunities to hear what other departments were doing. This increase in communication across departments was noted by a number of people as a positive unintended outcome of transitioning to a block schedule. Ultimately, one of the faculty members suggested that, as they looked at the additional space, perhaps they might want to include a large teacher planning room that would allow members of the various departments to mingle. The rationale was that the common planning space would encourage and facilitate communication across department teams. As a result of the suggestion, the staff did vote to provide teacher planning space as one large room situated near the teacher work room where all the equipment was housed. Within the large space, the department model was used, yet the low dividers between the departments allowed easy conversations to evolve.

Part of the success of the implementation of the block schedule is attributed to this serendipitous reaction. The planning in the teachers' room fostered increased communication among staff, resulting in many integrated curriculum designs and teaming models. The staff not only learned about using the more authentic teaching models recommended for the block, but also thrived on the collaborations with knowing colleagues.

■□■□■

Example: Institutionalizing the Innovation for Change

Another Illinois school maintains and supports two professional building initiatives that have become integral to the valued expectations of both old and new staff as part and parcel of their new teacher induction/orientation program. By including specific courses on working with block scheduling and on ways to differentiate teaching, initiatives have become institutionalized and continued with their initial and inherent integrity. All are on board, so to speak, and accountable for those things that are valued in that school's programs.

■ □ ■ □ ■

Chapter 3: Some Things We Know About Professional Development

After 20 years in the field, there are some things we know about professional development. We know about the evolution of professional development models, the value of building learning organizations, the elements of sound professional development, and the critical components of effective training models.

Evolution of Professional Development Models

To begin, we can follow the evolution of professional development models from the institute day, through district-wide professional development plans and site-based professional development to individualized professional learning.

The Institute Day

Historically, a common model of professional development was the one-day presentation. Sometimes referred to as the "dog and pony show," this model often is a presentation made by an expert or a team of experts. The one and only redeeming quality of one-shot programs is as an awareness session to initiate an innovation. Following the awareness, an interested cadre of learners is culled from the larger group for further professional development.

The one and only redeeming quality of one-shot programs is as an awareness session to initiate an innovation.

In another historic model, the institute day is designed as a smorgasbord of offerings, with teachers selecting their sessions, far in advance, and traveling around the district to their chosen session. This model has more appeal than the one-shot deal because of the options, but it is still a "dog and pony show" kind of day, lacking the follow-up of more comprehensive models.

District-Wide Professional Development Plan

A district-wide Professional Development Plan is a model that evolved in the early days of staff development because it was a natural way to introduce an entire faculty to an innovation. This model is sometimes referred to as the "spray paint method" or as some have said, "Spray and pray." Everyone has cooperative learning training. The entire district is exposed to theory of learning styles. Although this method works better than the one-shot deal because it usually involves multiple days over periods of time, it is still not sufficient training for full implementation without the key ingredients of practice, feedback, and coaching.

Well-designed strategic planning for on-going, continuous professional development is the hallmark of excellence in districts that target increased student achievement.

However, well-designed strategic planning for on-going, continuous professional development is the hallmark of excellence in districts that target increased student achievement. These plans are constructed with input from all the stakeholders and may be part of the district package for state and federal funding. Programs of excellence are job-embedded models, sustained over time, with practice, feedback, and coaching as integral elements.

■ □ ■ □ ■

Site-Based Professional Development

The concept of site-based professional development is training at the building level and is designed to be more responsive to school-wide goals that impact the whole staff. Effective site-based staff development operates within the parameters of an established, long-term staff development plan that often is filed at the district and state level. The strategic plan includes various innovations that often lead to both the general overall goals of the district and those that are specific to the school and its particular demographics and needs. The strategic plan model can be among the best when the leadership understands the facilitation processes of setting goals, obtaining buy-in by stakeholders, and building a community of learners. The drawback to this model is funding—a single school has a small budget. Often, several schools collaborate to create the needed funds for initiatives.

The strategic plan includes various innovations that often lead to both the general overall goals of the district and those that are specific to the school and its particular demographics and needs.

Individualized Professional Learning Plans

As a distinctive and fairly contemporary practice, Individualized Professional Learning Plans are becoming the norm in many school districts, as more states incorporate recertification requirements. In this model, each staff member is expected to plot a course of professional development opportunities, comprised of a specified number of clock hours and/or graduate credits that lead to state requirements for recertification. These opportunities range from traditional workshops to graduate course work to

■ □ ■ □ ■

mentoring responsibilities to action research in the classroom. Although approval of the professional development experiences remains at the district level, the individual teacher devises the actual plan with input, suggestions, and guidance from supervisory personnel. This model can be customized to the wants and needs of the individual as he or she determines an appropriate career path. The individualized plan becomes a package of growth and development tailored suitably to the talents and skills of the individual person. This plan offers a wide range of choices, but there is an expectation for rigor and relevance in the selections made.

> **The individualized plan becomes a package of growth and development tailored suitably to the talents and skills of the individual person.**

Summary

To summarize, professional development in a district often is comprised of all four described models. Yet, to have a program of integrity, strategic and long-term planning is always necessary. Districts are now beginning to work with systemic plans in place for professional development.

Learning Organizations

Lieberman (2000) writes about schools as learning organizations in which professional development is an integral part of everything that goes on in the school. In her discussion of effective models of learning organizations, she delineates the reasons why professional development often fails in its mission. The ten reasons, depicted in Figure 3.1, provide clear clues to some of the limitations that impede change through professional development practices.

Reasons Why Professional Development Fails

1. Lack of knowledge about how teachers learn
2. Teachers' definition of the problems of practice ignored
3. Agenda for reform not part of teachers' professional learning
4. Teaching described as set of technical skills, not invention
5. Importance of context within which teachers work is ignored
6. Support mechanisms and learning over time not considered
7. Time and mechanism for inventing often absent
8. Importance of facilitating at school level to change practice absent
9. Connection to school culture to change practice often ignored
10. Networks to support change in practice not promoted

Figure 3.1

In sum, the ten limitations cluster around the idea of lack of input on the part of key stakeholders, the teachers; initiatives introduced without sufficient context; and teacher creativity not considered as part of the process.

At the same time, Figure 3.1 provides insight into the power of learning communities. When educators know how teachers learn, when to involve them in generating the alternatives, when to foster creative solutions, and when to support them within the culture and the context of their work, the resulting response is positive and long-lasting. In fact, that is how real change occurs—over time and with the ownership of all directly involved.

■ □ ■ □ ■

In a similar vein, Schmoker (1996) advocates learning communities that are fairly flexible and informal but fiercely effective. He believes that the teacher team is the most powerful school improvement tool schools have. Schmoker believes that when teachers put their heads together and focus on an impending concern, uncovered and/or supported by data, they will find the best solutions because they are the ones closest to and most invested in the problem. His model has three parts, as listed in Figure 3.2: Managed Data, Meaningful Teams, and Measurable Goals/Standards.

Schmoker's School Improvement Model

Managed Data (Data): Student achievement data; demographics

Meaningful Teams (Dialogue): Grade level/department/vertical/core teams

Measurable Goals (Decision): Instructional/professional development goals

---

Figure 3.2

Briefly, this streamlined model consists of forming a team of teachers who work with the same group of students (creating meaningful teams). When formed, the team focuses on the most urgent achievement concerns revealed from on-going assessment data (data, dialogue phases). Then, based on the data, the on-going professional development dialogue, and the expertise of the team, goals are set, interventions are planned, and the plan is put into action (decision phase). Often, the instructional intervention requires specific professional development before the teachers are ready to fully implement the intervention. The entire process

The entire process of data, dialogue, and decision is a clear and simple methodology for school improvement, which works because the goal setting phase is focused on results.

■ □ ■ □ ■

of data, dialogue, and decision is a clear and simple methodology for school improvement, which works because the goal setting phase is focused on results.

Best Practices in Professional Development

As the field of professional development matures, the literature is filled with findings about what is and what is not effective in working with the adult learner. Among the many elements discussed in myriad journal articles and emerging research studies, there are five critical components that seem to spell success for substantive, long-lasting change. These five professional development attributes appear repeatedly in the literature and are supported by leading voices in this area of study. The following five adjectives describe rich, robust and rigorous models of professional learning (Figure 3.3): sustained, job-embedded, interactive, collegial, and integrated.

Professional Development: Five Critical Qualities

1. Sustained: training is implemented over time

2. Job-Embedded: training occurs and/or continues at the work site

3. Interactive: training invites, involves, and engages participants

4. Collegial: training builds and supports a community of learners

5. Integrated: training that is eclectic (Web-based, online, text, face-to-face)

Figure 3.3

A more detailed discussion is warranted. What do each of these qualities contribute? What does it look like and sound like to design skillful and sound professional development? How are the five elements related to each other and to the overall effectiveness of the process? To elaborate on the five qualities, each is defined with synonyms and described operationally through T-chart graphics to depict what they actually look and sound like.

Sustained Over Time

Sustained over time means that the professional development is ongoing and continual.

Sustained over time means that the professional development is ongoing and continual. It is a process that evolves over sufficient time for the participants to become acquainted with the basic ideas and to have time to work with the ideas in authentic and relevant ways and with the support of supervisory staff and colleagues (Figure 3.4).

Sustained Over Time

Looks Like	Sounds Like
Year-long or multiyear initiative	"It will be offered again in the summer and also in the fall."
School-wide and/or District-wide initiative	"We are starting with the Freshman program and will proceed through Grades10-12 programs, adding a grade each year."

Figure 3.4

Job-Embedded

Although the introductory sessions of the professional development experience may involve a centralized presentation at the district office, an integral part of the plan includes on-site, guided, and independent practice, supported by effective coaching and regular and specific feedback. In fact, on-site practice, rehearsal, and repetition of the skills and strategies in the classroom are critical to the overall success of the innovation (Figure 3.5).

An integral part of the plan includes on-site, guided, and independent practice, supported by effective coaching and regular and specific feedback.

Job-Embedded

Looks Like	Sounds Like
Classroom application of skills and/or strategies	"Your application was appropriate."
Peers coaching each other's work	"It worked well, but it needs better pacing."
Teachers observing each other	"I think that was the most effective part."

Figure 3.5

Interactive

Interactive professional development demonstrates the skillfulness of an effective facilitator, who knows how to invite participants to become involved and, sometimes, deeply engaged in the experience. This interactive model of adult learning features

Interactive professional development demonstrates the skillfulness of an effective facilitator.

the leader in the critical role of "guide on the side," with participants working collaboratively in pairs or in small groups (Figure 3.6).

Interactive

Looks Like	Sounds Like
Partners talking	"Form A/B partners."
Small groups working	"You will need a recorder and..."
Whole group activity	"Select the corner that best represents your position."

Figure 3.6

Collegial

Collegial models of professional development build on the concept on learning communities that bond in trusting relationships. Colleagues rely on each other and take on the roles of coach and cheerleader for the friends they are working with. Collegiality is what bonds the group of learners. It provides the emotional support for change as well as the expertise for developing the skills (Figure 3.7).

Colleagues rely on each other and take on the roles of coach and cheerleader for the friends they are working with.

■ □ ■ □ ■

Collegial

Looks Like	Sounds Like
Team meetings	Laughter, teasing and joking around
Friends helping friends	"I'll do that part."
Shared project or product	"I could never have done this without
Informal gatherings	your help."
	"It's been so helpful to have a partner."

Figure 3.7

Integrated

Integrated models of professional development are multimodal models that dictate an eclectic approach to adult learning. The experience might include Web-based learning, online interactions, traditional actions, text formats, or face-to-face instruction, but will usually use myriad approaches that appeal to a diverse adult learning population (Figure 3.8). As do young learners, adult learners need diversity and multimodal approaches. Each brain is different. Each responds to different stimuli.

Adult learners need diversity and multimodal approaches.

■□■□■

Integrated

Looks Like	Sounds Like
Research on the Web Classroom debriefings Buying "used text books"	"I love the chat room in this course." "I like the virtual office hours. It works for me." "I submitted my paper on line last night."

Figure 3.8

In sum, these five elements are the difference between professional development that works and professional development that fails. In the successful plan of professional development, meaningful applications are evident and effective. The results are long lasting, with continuing impact on student achievement. In the unsuccessful plan, the professional development often is a one-shot deal or a dog-and-pony show that is never actually applied and which results in, at best, spotty applications that are short-lived. The results in terms of student achievement are nonexistent or highly elusive. Thus, following the recognized design and including the elements that have emerged from the literature seem to be the logical choice for developing professional development plans.

> **In the successful plan of professional development, meaningful applications are evident and effective.**

The Training Model

This discussion focuses on the research-based best practices in the actual training model. As depicted in

Figure 3.9, the inverted triangle suggests the concept of drilling deep within the various aspects of working with adult learners. The figure begins with the broadest concept of the adult learning and change, narrows to the next concept of professional development, and finally, terminates with the most focused concept of the actual training. The reader may want to take a moment to reflect on the sequence in the figure.

Some Things We Know

THE ADULT LEARNER: THE CHANGE PROCESS

PROFESSIONAL
DEVELOPMENT

THE
TRAINING
MODEL

Figure 3.9

Leading voices in the field of training are Bruce Joyce and Beverly Showers (1995). Their research highlights the critical elements of effective training. In their classic text, *Student Achievement Through Staff Development*, they were among the first to discuss that elusive link between staff development activities in the staff room and increased student achievement in the classroom. They make that seemingly obvious connection that often eludes other educators leading the change process. For these educators, it is all too common that some type of professional development happens, yet there is no explicit expectation for positive results in terms of increased student achievement. Although the implicit goal is most certainly to realize change in student learning, making that actual connection to that goal is all too often overlooked.

> **Although the implicit goal is most certainly to realize change in student learning, making that actual connection to that goal is all too often overlooked.**

As this discussion unfolds, the training work of Joyce and Showers is the engine that runs the change train. Their now-infamous model, known by staff developers throughout the educational community, includes five major elements: theory, demonstration, practice, feedback, and coaching. Their training model is at the heart of the change process as initiatives are introduced into schools. Before proceeding, the reader may want to take a minute to rank the five elements according to the impact each has on professional development.

Each of the five elements is fully discussed separately. Figure 3.10, which shows the weight each element carries in the overall process, provides an easy comparison of the various elements as the reader analyzes the entirety of the training model.

The Training Model

Include THEORY	10% transfer in the classroom
And, add a DEMONSTRATION	10% transfer in the classroom
And, provide PRACTICE	10% transfer in the classroom
And, give specific FEEDBACK	15% transfer in the classroom
And, require on-site COACHING	80% transfer in the classroom

Figure 3.10

■ □ ■ □ ■

Theory

The first element is theory. Good, sound professional development establishes the theory base for the initiative by reviewing the research that supports the ideas manifested in the initiative. The theory becomes the scholarly citations that undergird the change initiative that is the focus of the training.

Attention to theory is basic to the change process. The theory base of research studies provides the needed rationale for the change initiative. The theory is what, ultimately, sparks the hope and the optimism that the change will create the intended difference in the targeted situation.

> **Attention to theory is basic to the change process.**

Although the element of theory is an integral part of the overall training model, it does not have to be the lead piece in the training. In fact, it usually is more effective to integrate the theory into the training a bit later in the process, after the participants have some level of understanding about the actual initiative. Skillful trainers have a sixth sense about when it seems most timely to introduce the theory base. In addition, they seem to sense what, when, and how much the group needs and/or wants, in terms of the theoretical underpinnings of the initiative, and they act accordingly.

> **Skillful trainers have a sixth sense about when it seems most timely to introduce the theory base.**

Perhaps a brief example of the impact that the theory portion of a training experience can have on the participants will help establish its importance. In Melbourne, Australia, the Master of Ceremonies of the Brain Conference kicked off the training with a short, but telling introduction of the keynote speaker, Howard Gardner, the founder and

developer of the highly acclaimed theory of multiple
intelligences. The emcee announced, "I'd like to introduce
you to Howard Gardner, the man who started it all, when
he added an "s" to the word intelligence." As he
finished, it was as quiet as a church service in the
enormous auditorium of 800 people. That was just what
they wanted to hear. They were there for the theory—
straight from the horse's mouth!

Demonstration

"Your actions speak so loudly, I can't hear your words" is
an adage that rings true in the training setting. The
demonstration is the action shot. It is the modeling that

**The demonstration
is the action shot.**

speaks loudly and clearly to all involved. This
demonstration element is presented in any
number of formats: live, face-to-face modeling;
video clips of the modeled behaviors; or the
display and discussion of authentic artifacts.

The demonstration portion of the training, as with
theory, is best when woven into the training. Sometimes,
beginning the session with a demonstration of the target
behavior is most effective. At other times, blending
demonstrations into the heart of the training material
immediately following an explanation of the behavior is
more appropriate. On other occasions, the flow of the
training material may dictate that demonstrations be used
toward the end of the presentation, as a conclusion to the
discussion that ensued.

However, regardless of timing, demonstrations are
essential to the training. This is the operational
component that models the theory with real examples,
showing what the initiative looks and sounds like. This is

the story of how it works, not just the declaration that it does work. The demonstration is the authentic look at the initiative in action and, sometimes, that action is modeled in myriad ways to fully illustrate its effectiveness in various scenarios.

Regardless of timing, demonstrations are essential to the training.

A quick example of the power of the demonstration element is illustrated in this story about a cooperative learning initiative. After four full days of training with a theory base and lots of interactive experiences in the sessions, participants revealed a startling fact: Many still did not know how they would go back to their schools and implement cooperative learning groups in their classrooms! In response to this concern, one of the leaders suggested watching a "home-grown'" video on cooperative learning. She explained that three teachers had videotaped their first cooperative learning lessons as models for other teachers in their school. To make a long story short (if it's not too late), the video showed three different classrooms (first grade, fourth grade, and sixth grade) with three different cooperative learning lessons. Each lesson clip was only about 4 to 5 minutes in length, yet the response from the training group was absolutely astonishing. Participants sighed with relief and said to each other and to the leaders, "Oh, we can do that. We know exactly what to do, now, after seeing cooperative groups in action." That is the power of a good demonstration!

■ □ ■ □ ■

Practice

Practice makes perfect? No, practice makes permanent!
Or, perfect practice makes perfect. Training with only
theory and demonstrations, no matter how powerful,
seldom yields relevant transfer or authentic applications
that have true and long-lasting impact.

> **Practice has to
> take place, and
> participants have
> to immerse
> themselves in
> actual trials of the
> initiative.**

Participants become empowered to actually use the
information in their home settings when they have some
amount of guided practice during the training
itself. Practice might be somewhat contrived,
perhaps using simulations or role playing;
abbreviated in terms of actual time needed;
and might even be sampled through one,
generic application. But, practice has to take
place, and participants have to immerse
themselves in actual trials of the initiative. They
have to experience the process, have
opportunities to ask questions, and have their concerns
addressed. They need some "hands-on time" with the
skills and strategies to get the feel of the process, to
operationalize abstract theory, and to have an opportunity
to experience what it actually looks and sounds like.

When a colleague attended a day-long software
training in the ballroom of a local hotel, he was
astonished to find that he was one of 450 other
participants. They were seated at long tables, with no
computers and no keyboards. The session included a
software demonstration, projected on the 12'X12'screen,
with a running monologue of the procedure. Participants
were expected to make notes in their three-ring binders,
with some questions allowed during the presentation. Yet,
because there was no hands-on component possible in this

setting, the learner left frustrated and unsure about how to actually use the complicated software package.

Feedback

A decisive component of the practice phase is feedback from the expert. Feedback is sometimes referred to as the "breakfast of champions" because relevant, specific feedback on a regular and periodic basis is how champions are made. Frequent, on-point feedback provides the necessary cues for continual refinements that move the learner from competent to proficient to expert.

> **Relevant, specific feedback on a regular and periodic basis is how champions are made.**

Feedback that is specific gives information that can be acted on. The more feedback there is and the more specific it is, the smoother the performance becomes. Feedback helps soften the rough edges. Practice with feedback provides fertile ground for improvements that make a difference. Practice with feedback completes the cycle of input and output. Feedback is the punctuation point at the end of the sentence, clarifying and providing closure to the performance.

> **Practice with feedback provides fertile ground for improvements that make a difference.**

It is natural to want feedback. Just watch kids at the swimming pool, diving and jumping and yelling. They're yelling to Mom, standing nearby, "Mom, watch this? How was that one? What did you think of that? Look, Mom, see this one." Every learner wants feedback from the authority figure, from the expert. They are trying their wings, and they want the expert's opinion on how well they flew. They want to hear words of

> **Every learner wants feedback from the authority figure.**

praise, but they will accept words of constructive criticism as they strive to perfect their performance.

Just as kids want the teacher's comment on the homework paper, adult learners want the instructor's mark of approval also. A simple story makes the point. A curriculum supervisor tells of using "walkthroughs and look-fors" in the classrooms, as a means of being accessible and available to the educators at four different buildings. To complete the routine, she would leave sticky notes in the teachers' mailboxes with a telling comment about what she had observed in the classroom. She often wondered if the process had the impact she intended — helping her connect to the teachers. Then, she found out. At a Parents' Night, one of the teachers' husbands confided to the supervisor that their refrigerator door was covered with the sticky notes she had given to his wife. Just like kids, this adult learner valued the feedback notes so much, she saved them and even put them on display on the refrigerator. Needless to say, the supervisor was surprised and pleased. It affirmed the method in her madness to connect with each teacher.

Coaching

Coaching is the on-site follow-up. It resembles feedback, but the difference is that coaching takes place on the job. It is job-embedded. This on-going, on-site coaching may consist of experts coaching novices or peers coaching each other. Yet, in either case, there is opportunity for immediate, specific refinement to the learner's performance. The coach provides the mirror to the adult learner and reflects, professionally, on the various elements of the

Coaching is the key to improving.

performance. Coaching in professional development is just like coaching in sports. It is someone telling someone what is working and what is not. Coaching is the key to improving.

Yet, coaching is sometimes considered the icing or the trimming on the cake, if you will, that adds extra charm to the overall product. It is not just the icing on the cake. It is the very element that makes the cake rise! Coaching is a fundamental element in a good training model. Without coaching, training does not take—it just does not work. Without coaching, the chances of any real application are slim at best. With coaching, transfer has an astonishingly good chance of occurring.

With coaching, transfer has an astonishingly good chance of occurring.

Figure 3.10, The Training Model, makes the point. It dramatically demonstrates through data the critical difference in training with a coaching element and training without a coaching element. If this chart is correct, and the authors have confidence that it is, then the undeniable conclusion becomes crystal clear. No training for professional development should ever occur if coaching is not available. Coaching must be required follow-up as an integral and necessary part to the entire process of change. The evidence is just too obvious. Without coaching, there is very little possibility of meaningful transfer and application. Training without coaching is simply a waste of time and money. Coaching is the critical link from the training site to the home site, be it classroom or business office.

Coaching is the critical link from the training site to the home site.

A classic example comes to mind that illustrates the skill and the finesse it takes to be an effective coach. Invited to a Texas ranch where her horses were stalled, a young woman suggested to her cousin that he might want to wander over to the riding corral to watch some lessons that were in progress. Sitting there, under a large, crooked shade tree, a seasoned horsewoman was quietly "coaching" three riders who circled around the corral, time after time. For each round, the coach made short, specific, and pointed suggestions to each rider:

"Sit tall!"

"Hug, with your knees!"

"Keep his head high!"

"You need a little more speed."

As each rider made the required adjustment, the coach continued with a steady stream of suggested shifts and changes to improve their performances. The goal was clearly to move each rider through the sequence of stages from novice to advanced beginner to competent rider to proficient horsewoman to expert showman to class champion. The coach's job was crystal clear. The coach was there to coach!

■□■□■

Chapter 4: Conclusion

Concerns Based Adoption Model

In closing, let's circle back to the concept of the adult learner. A classic study by Hall and Hord (1987), called Concerns Based Adoption Model (CBAM), focuses on the various concerns that adults experience in the process of change. According to their model, as depicted in Figure 4.1, as adults approach the impending change, they move along a spectrum of feelings that eventually lead to acceptance as they ultimately embrace the change.

Concerns Based Adoption Model

a. Aware
b. Information gathering
c. Personal
d. Task management
e. Impact on students
f. Collaboration to maximize impact
g. Refocusing and redirection

Figure 4.1

Before reading further, the reader may want to reflect on the various stages of acceptance and relate some of them to his or her personal experiences with change.

In the CBAM, Hall and Hord found that teachers experienced seven distinct levels of concern as they moved through the change process in adopting new material or new methods. In phase 1, Aware, they become aware of the impending change; then, in phase 2, Information Gathering, they become concerned with assembling information, wanting to find out about the impending change. In phase 3, Personal, teachers become concerned about what it means to them. In phase 4, Task Management, they start to think about how to do it. As they become familiar with the innovation, adult learners turn their attention to phase 5, Impact on Students, and begin to wonder what differences the change reveals. Along the path toward change, the adult learner eventually moves in phase 6, Collaboration, to maximize impact on students. In phase 7, Refocusing and Redirection, finally, adult learners come to the time when they move more fully into the innovation and refocus their concerns on skillful implementation and acceptance of the new material or new method.

It seems a wise and worthwhile effort to be familiar with the phases involved in the CBAM model for those who work as change agents with adult learners in professional development. Knowledge and understanding of their concerns can only lead to more insightful and inviting designs for change.

Situational Dispositions for Transfer

The model of transfer by Fogarty and Pete (2004) presents situational dispositions for transfer of learning for adult learners. In this model, six levels of transfer emerge, ranging from simple transfer (transfer that is close to the learning situation and is easy to apply to a new situation) to remote transfer (transfer that is far from the learning situation and requires mindfulness to apply). Although these six dispositions appear in each learner, their appearance varies by learning situations. Readers might recognize examples from their own learning experiences!

Six Levels of Transfer

Overlooks: Ollie, the Head-in-the-Sand Ostrich

Duplicates: Dan, the Drilling Woodpecker

Replicates: Laura, the Look-Alike Penguin

Integrates: Jonathon Livingston, the Seagull

Propagates: Cathy, the Carrier Pigeon

Innovates: Samantha, the Soaring Eagle

Figure 3.12

Overlooks: Ollie, the Head-in-the-Sand Ostrich

Beginning with the absence of transfer of any kind, Ollie depicts the learner who overlooks opportunities for transfer. This learner seems unaware of the relevance of the training and overlooks applications that may seem obvious to others. Ollie misses the point of the strategy or skill, as though the "shot didn't take." For example, after a tennis lesson that focused on how to grip the racket, the learner that is at the Ollie level of transfer ignores the newly presented procedure and persists in gripping the racket in the old way.

There is also the Ollie who intentionally overlooks or misses opportunities to use the new ideas. This learner transfer is characterized by the notion that the application is not worthy of doing. Most people have been Ollies at some point in their learning experiences, so this is not a judgmental model. It is a model of transfer with the goal of making learners more aware of their learning behavior.

Duplicates: Dan, the Drilling Woodpecker

Dan signifies the learner who drills and practices learning exactly as it was presented. The transfer becomes drill, drill, drill. This level of transfer is at an almost automatic stage. The learner does not move beyond copying the pattern. For example, the tennis player learns the steps and the swing for the backhand and practices the move faithfully until it is grooved. There is no attempt to personalize or customize the learning to fit the learner's needs better. Yet, this is a stab at transfer and application, to be celebrated.

Replicates: Laura, the Look-Alike Penguin

Laura is the learner who applies new learning in narrow ways, restricting the applications to one kind or one way, so the applications tend to all look alike. However, although transfer at this level is simple or near transfer, it does show indications of personalization. The learner tailors the idea in such a way that it works perfectly for her circumstances. This change or adjustment might be minor, but it is significant as it distinguishes this level from Dan, the Drilling Woodpecker at the duplicator level. Lauras adapt the new ideas in personally relevant ways. For example, a tennis player personalizes how he tosses the ball for the serve by using a particular pre-toss procedure that eventually becomes his trademark serving style.

Integrates: Jonathon Livingston, the Seagull

Jonathan Livingston, the Seagull, depicts the learner who
subtly integrates the new learning smoothly with former
ways. The transfer is implicit rather than explicit, and
Jonathan often says, "I already do this." This learner seems
to have a raised consciousness or acute awareness of the
learning, but is never really overt about the transfer.
Following the tennis example, this learner takes the strategy
of "playing the net" and seems to integrate the move directly
into the tennis game without explicit practice at the net. It is
a smooth, almost seamless, application, yet, perhaps, used
more frequently than before because of a raised
consciousness about its effectiveness.

Propagates: Cathy, the Carrier Pigeon

Cathy carries the new ideas to lots of new places, quite
intentionally. She maps the idea and "propagates" by
creating many new applications in many new situations.
Cathy is a natural learner, eager to find a use for what she
is learning. She is pragmatic and deliberate in her
applications. She often sees applications before the learning
is complete as she thinks ahead to how she might use some
idea. The tennis example might be that she learns about
terry headbands and wristbands to absorb the sweat during
play, and she immediately uses a headband in her aerobics
class. The next day, she uses a headband in her spinning
class and a week later, she uses a headband on her 5k "Run
for the Zoo." These are deliberate applications, creatively
propagated through many different activities because Cathy
has generalized the idea from the specific situation to other
similar situations.

Innovates: Samantha, the Soaring Eagle

Samantha illustrates the highest level and most complex kind of transfer. This learner leaps to transfer and beyond. She creates, invents, innovates, and enhances every idea with such elaboration, finesse, and grace that the original application is sometimes blurred. The transfer seems unique and is a metamorphosis of sorts. To look at an example with a tennis player, this learner takes the concept of a strategic play and outperforms her opponent with elaborate changes in pacing, positioning, and demeanor. The shifts in play become part of this player's repertoire and, over time, become part of the legend of this player's fame.

Further information about these models is available in the Nutshell book titled *A Look at Transfer: Seven Strategies That Work* (Fogarty & Pete, 2004).

Appendix: Discussion of Statements in Figure 1.1

Question 1. Adults seek learning experiences to cope with specific life-changing events. (True)

Discussion: Yes, this is true. Adult learners will seek learning opportunities in order to cope with job-related changes such as a promotion. They will seek new learning when stressed by changing family situations including divorce, a move, or an impending parent-care situation.

Case in Point: A professor once said, in a matter of fact way, "90% of female doctoral students are in a divorce or are newly divorced." That makes this point succinctly. Adults do seek learning to cope with major changes or disruptions in their lives.

Question 2. For adults, learning is its own reward. (True and False)

Discussion: True: Adults do learning-for-its-own-sake in areas of self-selected hobbies and interests. False: However, this is generally considered a false statement in terms of learning for or on the job. Adults seek to learn because there is an impending need in order to proceed along their chosen career paths. In the sense of seeking job learning for its own sake, the answer is not true.

Case in Point: Adults will pursue pleasurable learning to support their life style and to become more skillful as a gardener, a needle pointer, an artist, a gourmet cook, a musician, or even a "day trader." Yet, most learning for adults that is job-related is not done for its own reward, but rather because it is needed for advancement or maintaining the current job.

Question 3. Adults prefer survey courses to single concept courses. (False)

Discussion: The statement is false. Adult learners prefer to learn something in depth, rather than at a superficial, introductory, or awareness level.

They want to delve into the specifics of the learning with depth and understanding. They do not like to skim the surface generalities. They want specifics.

Case in Point: Adults want to pursue particular software training such as Excel, rather than taking a general course on office software.

Question 4: Adults want to use new materials. (False)

Discussion: Not so! Adult learners prefer the tried and true. They are frequently reluctant to switch to new materials, whether new software, new hardware, or new ideas. Adult learners epitomize two sayings, "It's hard to teach an old dog new tricks," and "You can lead a horse to water, but you can't make him drink."

Case in Point: Adults like the old comfortable shoes! They may come to the training to learn about the new information, but that doesn't mean they will actually embrace it or put it into practice.

Question 5: Adults are quick to re-evaluate old materials. (False)

Discussion: Paralleling the previous statement, adults do not easily give up the old materials. They tend to hang on to them and continue to use them when they can. If they are "forced" to move into the new material, they may still retain much of the old or they gradually and cautiously weave the new into their existing repertoire. It is usually a slow process in which adult learners eventually achieve a level of confidence that allows them to move forward.

Case in Point: Textbook adoptions cause great concern for teachers. They do not want to give up their well-worn units for their favorite activities.

In another example, the executive of a small publishing company, in an attempt to get everyone computer literate, banned the use of typewriters in the office. Although the office team followed orders, on the surface, the entire staff conspired to keep one lone typewriter in the storeroom for "emergencies." In their mind, "emergencies" occurred every time someone needed to type an address on an envelope, a skill they had not conquered yet on the computer.

Question 6: Adults prefer to learn alone. (False)

Discussion: Nope! Adults like working with others. They thrive in collaboration with a colleague and in the dialogue process that ensues. Adult learners become quite reflective as learning partners or learning teams.

Case in Point: Most distance learning models are designed with a collaborative component so adult learners can dialogue with a buddy or partner and feel a sense of support.

Question 7: Adults prefer "sit and gits." (False)

Discussion: Adult learners want a collaborative, interactive hands-on learning experience. They want to try things in step-by-step procedural ways. Adults are eager to do whatever it is they are learning to do, and they want to try it out with an expert nearby.

Case in Point: A friend attended a software training that was conducted in a hotel ballroom with 450 people in attendance. No one had a computer to use except the instructor, who projected the performance sequence on a 12 x 12 screen. My friend's appraisal of the experience was that "it was the worst seminar I have ever attended."

Question 8: Adults prefer "how to" trainings. (True)

Discussion: Absolutely! Adult learners want the nuts and bolts! They want to know specifically "how to" manage the task or skill they are learning. Adult learners are eager to know all about the practical components so that they can practice them and take them back to their work setting with ease and grace.

Case in Point: When learning to play golf, the novice does not really care that much about the history of the game itself, about the metaphors, the equipment, or the rules. They want to know how to grip the club, which club to grip, and how to drive, chip, and putt. They want the nitty-gritty pieces.

Question 9: An eclectic approach works best with the adult learner. (True)

Discussion: Yes! Focus groups often reveal preferences of adult learners that include a combination of online and work-based and the more traditional face-to-face interactions.

Case in Point: Many field-based or distance learning programs in education require intermittent on-site retreats — either over a weekend or during the summer holidays.

Question 10: Non-human learning (books, TV) is popular in adult learning. (True)

Discussion: Although adult learners relish collaboration and face-to-face dialogue, they also, at times, embrace non-human forms of learning. Books, television, and the Internet are popular sources of information for adult learners.

Case in Point: Adult viewers cite *Band of Brothers*, an eight-part docudrama on HBO about World War II, as the greatest tool for clarifying the historical event.

Question 11: Adults don't like problem-centered learning. (False)

Discussion: No! Just the opposite is true. Adults are hooked into learning situations through the skill of appropriate and personally relevant real-world problems. By presenting scenarios of actual situations, adult learners are attracted to the problem and immediately get into problem-solving mode.

Case in Point: The vignettes in case studies of schools provide fertile ground for leadership seminars during which practical problem solving becomes the rule resulting in rich discussions.

Question 12: Adults carry reservoirs of personal experience. (True)

Discussion: So true! Adult learners are laden with myriad experiences that they bring to the learning setting. In fact, the expression "lesson learned" is critical to the learning process. As new information comes in, adult brains search for patterns that fit. By attaching the new to former or existing information, adult learners actually internalize the learning for storage with long-term memory. Adult learners tend to pursue learning along the lines of career interests that will eventually translate into job advancement or life fulfillment. Thus, adult learners are often building on an existing knowledge base that can be both rich and diverse.

Case on Point: An estate-planning attorney seeks accounting and tax seminars that can continue to build and update her knowledge base for her primary business in estate planning.

Question 13: "Real world" exercises are preferred. (True)

Discussion: This is true. Adult learners want actual situations to ponder and problems to solve. They do not especially like the "fantasy" problems as evidenced by their reluctance to dig in with this kind of problem; instead, they turn off.

Case in Point: Middle school teachers will complain, "But this is not realistic. This would never happen. It's not useful to spend time on these hypothetical situations, no school schedule allows for this kind of time for 'advisory programs'."

Question 14: Adults let their schoolwork take second place to jobs and family. (True)

Discussion: The bad news is yes, they do. The good news is they do it because they are clear about their responsibilities. But, because they see learning as part of those responsibilities, their school work does get done, too.

■□■□■

Case in Point: Many a mom spends quality time and energy with family affairs, including errands, soccer practice, dinner, and housework before she settles down, late in the evening, to the reading required for her graduate classes.

Question 15: Adults transfer ideas and skills easily into their work settings. (False)

Discussion: Adults do not always see the application to their work. When the learning is closely related to work in the case of a newly learned skill, only then is the transfer ready-made. More often than not, with complex processes, transfer requires explicit coaching and much "shepherding" to be skillfully applied.

Case in Point: Adults usually can move between a PC and a Mac computer with little effort. Yet, they may experience great difficulty in changing from one operating system to another. The operating systems are often conceptually quite different; therefore, the transfer must be more mindful.

Question 16: Adults are self-directed learners. (True)

Discussion: True! True! Adults are usually clear and focused about what they want to achieve. They select the right program for them to meet their specific goals in terms of time constraints, effort and outcomes.

Case in Point: Second-career teachers seek out an expedient university program that offers the course work needed, the necessary practicum, and the alternative certification required to actually be placed in a school for a teaching position.

Question 17: Facilitation of groups works better that lecture format with adult learners. (True)

Discussion: Adults want to experience learning with real and authentic activities. They want to collaborate and discuss their work and form reasoned judgments about how they are doing. For adults, working in groups gives them a chance to dialogue with other learners to confirm understanding and to discuss process.

Case in Point: A well-run training session at a local bank involves the participants in case study scenarios as it teaches customer service skills.

Question 18: Adults expect their class time to be well spent. (True)

Discussion: An adamant yes! Time is precious! Adults do not want their "valuable time" wasted in inefficient or superfluous ways. They are committed to a certain amount of time for class and they want it to be well spent.

Case in Point: One graduate student habitually complained to a professor who regularly dismissed the class early, while the undergraduates were ecstatic! The adult learner wanted to "get everything" he could possibly get in his time with the teacher.

Question 19: Adults are voluntary, self-directed learners. (True)

Discussion: Yes, in many cases, adults seek learning situations they want or need and voluntarily attend to their school responsibilities. Yet, in some cases, they are volunteering only to fill a requirement for certification or advancement.

Case in Point: A golf pro voluntarily attends the required hours of PGA classes needed annually to retain certain levels of certification.

Question 20: Adults are pragmatic learners. (True)

Discussion: Oh, yes! The picture by now, after nineteen previously discussed traits, is becoming quite clear. Adult learners are learning for a reason. They are focused, tenacious, and goal-oriented. Adult learners want to cross the finish line and go on with their lives!

Case in Point: Many adult learners accelerate their doctoral programs and complete the course work in record time. They are eager to get on with the real work— the dissertation.

Bibliography

Backer, L., Deck, M., & McCallum, D. (1995). *The presenter's survival kit. It's a jungle out there.* St. Louis, MO: Mosby-Year Book.

Bellanca, J. (1990). *The cooperative think tank: Graphic organizers to teach thinking in the cooperative classroom.* Thousand Oaks, CA: Corwin.

Bellanca, J. (1992). *The cooperative think tank: Graphic organizers to teach thinking in the cooperative classroom.* Thousand Oaks, CA: Corwin.

Bellanca, J. (1995). *Designing professional development for change.* Thousand Oaks, CA: Corwin.

Bellanca, J., & Fogarty, R. (2003). *Blueprints for achievement in the cooperative classroom* (2nd ed.). Thousand Oaks, CA: Corwin.

Birnie, W. (1999). 7 deadly sins. *Journal of Staff Development,* 65–68.

Burke, K. (1997). *Designing professional portfolios for change.* Thousand Oaks, CA: Corwin.

Cordeiro, P., Kraus, C., & Binkowski, K. (1997, March). *A problem-based learning approach to professional development: Supporting learning for transfer.* Paper presented at the Annual Meeting of the American Educational Research Association, Chicago, IL.

DeBoer, A. (1986). *The art of consulting.* Chicago: Arcturus Books.

■□■□■

Dietz, M. (1998). *Journals as frameworks for change.* Thousand Oaks, CA: Corwin.

Fogarty, R. (1991). *How to integrate the curricula.* Thousand Oaks, CA: Corwin.

Fogarty, R. (1997). *Brain compatible classrooms.* Thousand Oaks, CA: Corwin.

Fogarty, R. (2000). *Ten things new teachers need to succeed.* Thousand Oaks, CA: Corwin.

Fogarty, R. (2001a). *A model for mentoring our teachers: Centers of pedagogy.* Chicago: Fogarty & Associates.

Fogarty, R. (2001b). *Finding the time and the money for professional development.* Chicago: Fogarty & Associates.

Fogarty, R. (2001c). Roots of change. *Journal of Staff Development, 34–36.*

Fogarty, R., & Pete, B. M. (2004). *A look at transfer: Seven strategies that work.* Thousand Oaks, CA: Corwin.

Fullan, M., & Stiegelbauer, E. (1991). *The new meaning of educational change.* New York: Teachers College.

Garmston, R. J., & Wellman, B. M. (1992). How to make presentations that teach and transform. *The School Administrator, 36–38.*

Garvin, D. A. (2000). *Learning into action: A guide to putting the learning organization to work.* Cambridge, MA: Harvard Business School Press.

Gousie, G. (1997, May). *Speaking with confidence.* Paper presented at the National Head Start Association, Boston, MA.

■□■□■

Grant, J., & Forsten, C. (1999). *If you're riding a horse and it dies, get off.* Peterbourough, NH: Crystal Springs Books.

Guskey, T. (2000) *Evaluating professional development.* Thousand Oaks, CA: Corwin.

Hall, G., & Hord, S. (1987). *Change in schools, facilitating the process.* Albany: State University of New York.

Hargreaves, A. (1994). *Changing teachers, changing times: Teacher's work and culture in the post modern age.* New York: Teachers College Press.

Hoff, R. (1998). *I can see you naked: A fearless guide to making great presentations.* New York: Andrews & McMeel.

Johnson, D. W., Johnson, R. T., & Holubec, E. J. (1986). *Circles of learning: Cooperation in the classroom.* Alexandria, VA: Association for Supervision and Curriculum Development.

Johnson, D. W., Johnson, R. T., & Holubec, E. J. (1998). *Cooperation in the classroom.* Edina, MN: Interaction Book Company.

Johnson, S. (1998). *Who Moved My Cheese?* New York: Putnam's Sons.

Johnson, S. (1998). *Who Moved My Cheese?* [Audiotape]. New York: Simon & Schuster.

Joyce, B., & Showers, B. (1983). *Power in staff development through research on training.* Alexandria, VA: Association for Supervision and Curriculum Development.

Joyce, B., & Showers, B. (1995). *Student achievement through staff development.* White Plaines, NY: Longman.

■□■□■

Killion, J. (1999). Knowing when and how much to steer the ship. *Journal of Staff Development, 59–60.*

Knowles, M. (1973). *The adult learner: A neglected species.* Houston, TX: Gulf Professional Publishing.

Knowles, M., Holton, E., & Swanson, R. (1998). *The adult learner: The definitive classic in adult education and human resource development* (5th ed.). Woburn, MA: Butterworth-Heinemann.

Krupp, J. (1981). *Adult development: Implications for staff development.* Manchester, CT: Author.

Krupp, J. (1982). *The adult learner: A unique entity.* Manchester, CT: Author.

Lieberman, A., & Miller, L. (2000). Teaching and teacher development: A synthesis for a new century. In R. S. Barth, *Education in a new era.* Alexandria, VA: Association for Supervision and Curriculum Development.

Little, J. W. (1975). The power of organizational setting: School norms and staff development. Paper adapted from final report to the National Institute on Education, *School success and staff development: The role of staff development in urban desegregated schools,* 1981.

Moye, V. (1997). *Conditions that support transfer for change.* Arlington Heights, IL: Skylight Training and Publishing.

Pike, R., & Arch, D. (1997). *Dealing with difficult participants.* San Francisco: Jossey-Bass.

Radin, J. (1998.) So, you want to be an educational consultant? *The School Administrator,* February, 1998.

Sarasan, S. (1982). The *culture of school and the problem of change* (2nd ed.). Boston: Allyn & Bacon.

■ □ ■ □ ■

Scearce, C. (1992). *100 ways to build teams.* Thousand Oaks, CA: Corwin.

Schmoker, M. (1996) *Results: The key to continuous school improvement.* Alexandria, VA:. Association of Supervision and Curriculum Development.

Schmuck, R. (1997). *Practical action research for change.* Arlington Heights, IL: Skylight Training and Publishing.

Schmuck, R., & Schmuck, P. (1997). *Group processes in the classroom.* Madison, WI: Brown and Benchmark.

Sparks, D., & Loukes-Horsley, S. (1990). *Five models of staff development.* Oxford, OH: National Staff Development Council.

Stern, N., & Payment, M. (1995). *101 stupid things trainers do to sabotage success.* Irvine, CA: Richard Chang Associates.

Tate, M. (in press). *Lessons learned: 20 instructional strategies that engage the adult mind.* Thousand Oaks, CA: Corwin.

Van Ekeren, G. (1994). *Speaker's sourcebook II: Quotes, stories and anecdotes for every occasion.* Paramus, NJ: Prentice Hall.

Wang, N., & Taraban, R. (1997). *Do learning strategies affect adults' transfer of learning?* (ERIC Document Reproduction Service No. ED413 419)

Williams, R. B. (1996). Four dimensions of the school change facilitator. *Journal of Staff Development,* 48–50.

Williams, R. B. (1996). *More than 50 ways to build team consensus* [Training Package]. Thousand Oaks, CA: Corwin.

■ □ ■ □ ■

Williams, R. B. (1997). *Twelve roles of the facilitator for school change*. Thousand Oaks, CA: Corwin.

Wohlsletter, P. (1997). *Organizing for successful school-based management*. Alexandria, VA: Association of Supervision and Curriculum Development.

Zemke, R., & Zemke, S. (1995). Adult learning: What do we know for sure? *Training Magazine*, 31–40.

■ □ ■ □ ■